Oh, What Nonsense!

poems selected by **WILLIAM COLE**

drawings by **TOMI UNGERER**

Oh,

What Nonsense!

THE VIKING PRESS   **NEW YORK**

SBN 670–05025–3

Text Copyright © 1966 by William Cole

Illustrations Copyright © 1966 by Tomi Ungerer

ALL RIGHTS RESERVED

Viking Seafarer edition issued in 1969 by The Viking Press, Inc.
625 Madison Avenue, New York, N.Y. 10022

Library of Congress catalog card number: AC 66–10249

821.08; 808.81 1. *Children's poetry*
2. *Nonsense verses*

PRINTED IN U.S.A.

2   3   4   5   6   76   75   74   73   72

Acknowledgement is made to the following for permission to use material owned by them. Every reasonable effort has been made to clear the use of the poems in this volume with the copyright owners. If notified of any omissions, the editor and publisher will gladly make the proper corrections in future editions.

Appleton-Century, for "Jumble Jingle" and "Tom Tickleby and His Nose" from *I Have a Song to Sing You* by Laura Richards, Copyright 1938 by Appleton-Century Co., Inc.; and for "Merry Thoughts" from *Merry-go-round* by Laura E. Richards.

Atlantic—Little, Brown and Co., for "Cow" from *Blue Boy's Book of Beasts* by William Jay Smith, Copyright © 1956, 1957 by William Jay Smith.

Beatrice Curtis Brown, for "A New Song to Sing about Jonathan Bing" by Beatrice Curtis Brown, published by Oxford University Press, Copyright 1936–1964 by Beatrice Curtis Brown.

Dennis Dobson, London, for "On the Ning Nang Nong" and "A Thousand Hairy Savages" from *Silly Verse for Kids* by Spike Milligan.

The Dolphin Publishing Company, Limited, for "Tragedy" from *Life Through Young Eyes* by W. Cheney.

Doubleday & Company, Inc., for "Dinky," Copyright 1953 by Theodore Roethke from the book *Words for the Wind* by Theodore Roethke; and for "The Lizard," Copyright © 1961 by Theodore Roethke from the book *I Am! Says the Lamb* by Theodore Roethke.

E. P. Dutton & Co., Inc., for "Mr. Kartoffel" from the book *The Wandering Moon* by James Reeves, published 1960 by E. P. Dutton & Co., Inc.; and for "Sir Smasham Uppe" from the book *The Flattered Flying Fish and Other Poems* by E. V. Rieu, Copyright © 1962 by E. V. Rieu.

Houghton Mifflin Company, for "The Man in the Onion Bed" from John Ciardi's *I Met a Man*, Copyright © 1961 by John Ciardi, published by Houghton Mifflin Company.

"The Happy Family" copyright © 1961 The Curtis Publishing Company. "The Happy Family" is from the book *The Man Who Sang the Sillies* by John Ciardi. Copyright © 1961 by John Ciardi. Reprinted by permission of J. B. Lippincott Company.

Little, Brown and Co., for "The Folk Who Live in Backward Town " from *Hello and Good-by* by Mary Ann Hoberman, Copyright © 1959 by Mary Ann and Norman Hoberman; for "Just Because" from *Take Sky* by David McCord, Copyright 1961, 1962 by David McCord; and for "The Buffalo" from *Tirra Lirra* by Laura E. Richards, Copyright 1932 by Laura E. Richards.

The Macmillan Company, for "Don't Ever Seize a Weasel by the Tail," reprinted with permission of The Macmillan Company from *A Gopher in the Garden* by Jack Prelutsky, Copyright © 1966, 1967 by Jack Prelutsky.

Methuen & Co., Ltd., for "Old Mr. Bows" from *Clinkerdump* by Wilma Horsbrugh.

Oxford University Press, London, for "The Tickle Rhyme" from *The Tale of the Monster Horse* by Ian Seraillier.

Pantheon Books, a Division of Random House, Inc., for "The Contrary Waiter" from *Stuff and Nonsense* by Edgar Parker, Copyright 1961 by Edgar Parker.

Jack Prelutsky, for his poem "From the Sublime to the Ridiculous to the Sublimely Ridiculous to the Ridiculously Sublime."

Shel Silverstein, for his poems "Beware, My Child," "Boa Constrictor," and "Mr. Spats."

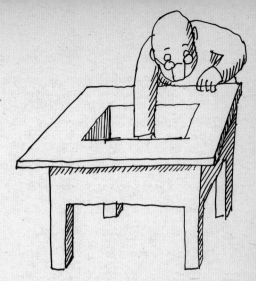

Contents

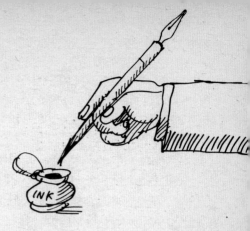

Introduction

Imagine a hippopotamus with soft blue eyes! Or a barefoot boy with shoes on! Or an antelope eating a cantaloupe! Oh, what nonsense! Such things just don't happen.

And what a pity it is that they don't. But at least people write about such silly things; that's something to be thankful for. The word "nonsense," of course, means "no sense"—and that is exactly what all these poems have—no sense. Just as people who have no sense are usually quite happy, these no-sense poems are happy. They are like jumps of joy—imagine someone walking quietly along, and suddenly he feels like jumping up in the air and doing a little dance. They're expressions of joy; little dances danced for no reason except for the fun of it.

There are other words for nonsense, and some of them almost make you laugh just hearing them: shenanigans, twiddle-twaddle, fiddle-faddle, monkeyshines, balderdash, bushwa, doggerel, poppycock, and flapdoodle. Some of these are very old words, for people were making up nonsense in rhyme centuries back; in fact, much of Mother Goose is sheer nonsense. Some of the poems in this book are jump-rope rhymes and counting-out rhymes

9

made up by children; others are words to songs. We don't know who wrote some of the poems; the authors didn't sign their names, or else the poems weren't written down, but passed by memory from person to person. When we don't know who wrote something, we say it is "anonymous," which is a Greek word meaning "nameless." So remember:

> Don't miss your chance for wealth and fame;
> When you write something funny, sign your name.

Now someone who is a moldy fig, or a wet smack, or a noodle-head, is sure to say about this book: "Oh, what nonsense! Here's a book of nonsense poems with no poems in it by Edward Lear or Lewis Carroll!" And they're right, but these two great nonsense poets are left out on purpose; they can be found in hundreds of other books—and I hope you will look for them in other books—but mostly they're left out because I wanted to use my space for things you can't find anywhere else. So if anyone says to you, "Oh, what nonsense! No Lear or Carroll!" you tell them for me: "Fiddle-faddle! Twiddle-twaddle! Bushwa! And balderdash!"

WILLIAM COLE

Beware, My Child

Beware, my child,
of the snaggle-toothed beast.
He sleeps till noon,
then makes his feast
on Hershey bars
and cakes of yeast
and anyone around—o.

So when you see him,
sneeze three times
and say three loud
and senseless rhymes
and give him all your
saved-up dimes,
or else you'll ne'er be found—o.

SHEL SILVERSTEIN

The Folk Who Live in Backward Town

The folk who live in Backward Town
Are inside out and upside down.
They wear their hats inside their heads
And go to sleep beneath their beds.
They only eat the apple peeling
And take their walks across the ceiling.

MARY ANN HOBERMAN

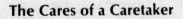

The Cares of a Caretaker

A nice old lady by the sea
    Was neat as she was plain,
And every time the tide came in
    She swept it back again.

And when the sea untidy grew
    And waves began to beat,
She took her little garden rake
    And raked it smooth and neat.

alone

She ran a carpet-sweeper up
    And down the pebbly sand.
She said, "This is the only way
    To keep it clean—good land!"

And when the gulls came strolling by,
    She drove them shrilly back,
Remarking that it spoiled the beach,
    "The way them birds do track."

She fed the catfish clotted cream
   And taught it how to purr—
And were a catfish so endowed
   She would have stroked its fur.

She stopped the little sea urchins
   That traveled by in pairs,
And washed their dirty faces clean
   And combed their little hairs.

She spread white napkins on the surf
   With which she fumed and fussed.
"When it ain't covered up," she said,
   "It gits all over dust."

She didn't like to see the ships
　　With all the waves act free,
And so she got a painted sign
　　Which read: "Keep off the Sea."

But dust and splutter as she might,
　　Her work was sadly vain;
However oft she swept the beach,
　　The tides came in again.

And she was sometimes wan and worn
　　When she retired to bed—
"A woman's work ain't never done,"
　　That nice old lady said.

WALLACE IRWIN

Some Families of My Acquaintance

The Rummy-jums, the Rummy-jums,
  Are very funny people;
(Very, very, very, very,
  Very funny people!)
They run as hard as they can go,
  And clamber up the steeple;

(Clamber-climber, climber-clamber,
   Clamber up the steeple!)
And when they get up to the top,
They say, "Good gracious, we must stop!"
And turn about with grief and pain,
And clamber-climber down again.

The Viddipocks, the Viddipocks,
   Have very pretty bonnets;
(Very, very, very, very,
   Very pretty bonnets!)
And when they wear them upside down,
   They write most lovely sonnets;
(Lovely-dovely, dovely-lovely,
   Lovely-dovely sonnets!)
And sitting on the new-mown hay,
They wirble-warble all the day;
"For oh," they say, "at such a time,
Our very ribbons flow in rhyme!"

The Wiggle-wags, the Wiggle-wags,
   They never know their mind, sir;
(Never, never, never, never,
   Never know their mind, sir!)
Sometimes they hook their frocks before,
   And sometimes up behind, sir;
(Hook them, crook them, crook them, hook them,
   Hook them up behind, sir!)
And first they turn them inside out,
Then outside-inside with a shout;
"For oh," they say, "there's no one knows
Which way the most our beauty shows!"

LAURA E. RICHARDS

A Thousand Hairy Savages

A thousand hairy savages
Sitting down to lunch
Gobble gobble glup glup
Munch munch munch.

SPIKE MILLIGAN

The Minister in the Pulpit

The minister in the pulpit,
He couldn't say his prayers,
He laughed and he giggled,
And he fell down the stairs.
The stairs gave a crack,
And he broke his humphy back,
And all the congregation
Went "Quack, quack, quack!"

SCOTTISH NURSERY RHYME

Way Down South Where Bananas Grow

Way down South where bananas grow,
A grasshopper stepped on an elephant's toe.
The elephant said, with tears in his eyes,
"Pick on somebody your own size!"

ANONYMOUS

The Man in the Onion Bed

I met a man in an onion bed.
He was crying so hard his eyes were red.
And the tears ran off the end of his nose
As he ate his way down the onion rows.

He ate and he cried, but for all his tears
He sang: "Sweet onions, oh my dears!
I love you, I do, and you love me,
But you make me as sad as a man can be."

JOHN CIARDI

The Contrary Waiter

A tarsier worked as a waiter.
He wore a stiff collar and tie.
He said, "Of all creatures who cater,
None are calm and undaunted as I."

When asked to serve mutton with mustard,
He'd scribble a note on a pad
And return with a half-eaten custard
And say it was all that they had.

When a cup of hot cocoa was ordered,
His eyes would defiantly gleam;
He'd bring back asparagus bordered
With heaps of vanilla ice cream.

If cucumber salad was wanted,
The customer suffered a shock:
The tarsier, calm and undaunted,
Brought rice pudding, stuffed in a sock.

He never brought what was requested.
There was always a terrible risk.
And customers—if they protested—
Were splattered with hot oyster bisque.

One day an immense alligator
Sat down at a table to sup.
He grabbed the contemptible waiter
And ate him contemptibly up.

EDGAR PARKER

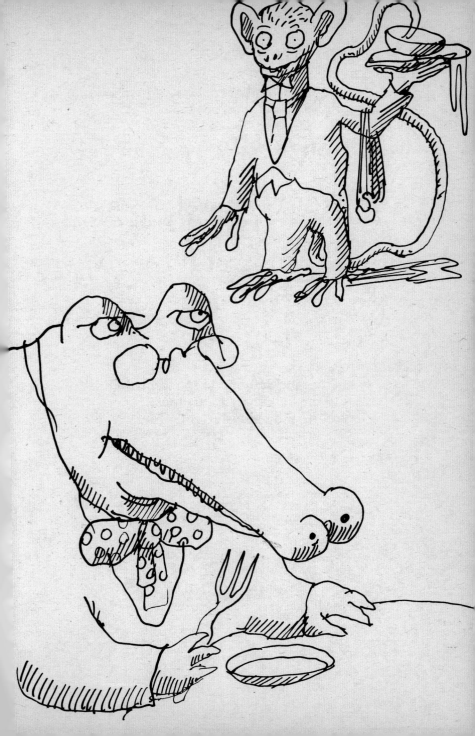

From the Sublime to the Ridiculous to the Sublimely Ridiculous to the Ridiculously Sublime

An antelope eating a cantaloupe
is surely a strange thing to see,
but a cantaloupe eating an *antelope*
is something that never will be.

(And an *antelope* eating an antelope
is a thing that can hardly befall,
but a *cantaloupe* eating a *cantaloupe*—
well, that *never* could happen at all!)

JACK PRELUTSKY

26

Dinky

O what's the weather in a Beard?
It's windy there, and rather weird,
And when you think the sky has cleared
   —Why, there is Dirty Dinky.

Suppose you walk out in a Storm,
With nothing on to keep you warm,
And then step barefoot on a Worm
   —Of course, it's Dirty Dinky.

As I was crossing a hot hot Plain,
I saw a sight that caused me pain.
You asked me before,
I'll tell you again:
   —It *looked* like Dirty Dinky.

Last night you lay a-sleeping?
No! The room was thirty-five below;
The sheets and blankets turned to snow.
   —He'd got in: Dirty Dinky.

You'd better watch the things you do,
You'd better watch the things you do.
You're part of him; he's part of you
   —*You* may be Dirty Dinky.

THEODORE ROETHKE

27

Boa Constrictor

Oh I'm being eaten by a boa constrictor,
A boa constrictor, a boa constrictor,
I'm being eaten by a boa constrictor,
And I don't like it . . . one bit!
Well what do you know . . . it's nibbling my toe,
Oh gee . . . it's up to my knee,
Oh my . . . it's up to my thigh,
Oh fiddle . . . it's up to my middle,
Oh heck . . . it's up to my neck,
Oh dread . . . it's . . . MMFFF.

SHEL SILVERSTEIN

Advice to Children

For a domestic, gentle pet,
A hippopotamus I'd get—
　　　They're very kind and mild.
I'm sure if you but purchase one
You'll find 'twill make a lot of fun
　　　For any little child.

Select one of a medium size,
With glossy fur and soft blue eyes,
　　　Then brush and comb him well.
With wreaths of flowers his forehead deck,
And from a ribbon round his neck
　　　Suspend a silver bell.

If it should be a rainy day,
Up in the nursery he will play
　　　With Baby, Tot and Ted;
Upon the rocking-horse he'll ride,
Or merrily he'll run and hide
　　　Beneath a chair or bed.

And when he wants to take a nap,
He'll cuddle up in Totty's lap,
　　　As quiet as a mouse.
Just try it, and you'll soon agree
A hippopotamus should be
　　　A pet in every house.

CAROLYN WELLS

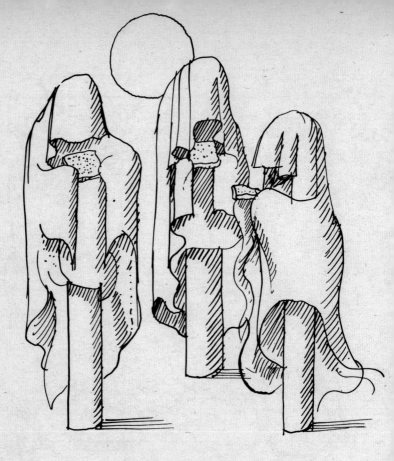

There Were Three Ghostesses

There were three ghostesses
Sitting on postesses
Eating buttered toastesses
And greasing their fistesses
Right up to their wristesses.
Weren't they beastesses
To make such feastesses!

ANONYMOUS

There Was a Young Lady Residing at Prague

There was a young lady residing at Prague,
Whose ideas were really most wonderfully vague.
When anyone said to her: "What a fine day!"
"Roast chicken is nice," she would dreamily say,
"And a mushroom on toast is the very best thing
To make a canary or hummingbird sing."
The people of Prague thought this conduct so strange,
They quickly decided she needed a change,
So packed her with care in a box with some hay,
And paid her expenses as far as Bombay.

ANONYMOUS

The Happy Family

Before the children say goodnight,
　　Mother, Father, stop and think:
Have you screwed their heads on tight?
　　Have you washed their ears with ink?

Have you said and done and thought
　　All that earnest parents should?
Have you beat them as you ought:
　　Have you begged them to be good?

And above all—when you start
　　Out the door and douse the light—
Think, be certain, search your heart:
　　Have you screwed their heads on tight?

If they sneeze when they're asleep,
　　Will their little heads come off?
If they just breathe very deep?
　　If—especially—they cough?

Should—alas!—the little dears
　　Lose a little head or two,
Have you inked their little ears:
　　Girls' ears pink and boys' ears blue?

Children's heads are very loose.
　　Mother, Father, screw them tight.
If you feel uncertain use
　　A monkey wrench, but do it right.

If a head should come unscrewed
   You will know that you have failed.
Doubtful cases should be glued.
   Stubborn cases should be nailed.

Then when all your darlings go
   Sweetly screaming off to bed,
Mother, Father, you may know
   Angels guard each little head.

Come the morning you will find
   One by one each little head
Full of gentle thoughts and kind,
   Sweetly screaming to be fed.

JOHN CIARDI

Cinderella

Cinderella,
Dressed in yella,
Went downtown
To buy some mustard;
On the way
Her girdle busted—
How many people
Were disgusted?
One-two-three-four-five-six-seven ...

COUNTING-OUT RHYME

The Lizard

The Time to Tickle a Lizard
Is Before, or Right After, a Blizzard.
Now the place to begin
Is just under his Chin,—
And here's more Advice:
Don't Poke more than Twice
At an Intimate Place like his Gizzard.

THEODORE ROETHKE

One Two Three

One two three
   Father caught a flea:
Put him in the teapot
   To make a cup of tea.

ANONYMOUS

Just Because...

Kittens have paws they don't have pawses,
Lions have maws they don't have mawses,
Tigers have jaws they don't have jawses,
And crows have caws they don't have cawses.

I make one pause, I make two pauses:

Nine jackdaws aren't nine jackdawses,
Seven seesaws aren't seven seesawses,
Five oh pshaws aren't five oh pshawses,
Three heehaws aren't three heehawses.

Do you give two straws? Do you give two strawses?

DAVID McCORD

The Boy Stood in the Supper-room

The boy stood in the supper-room
 Whence all but he had fled;
He'd eaten seven pots of jam
 And he was gorged with bread.

"Oh, one more crust before I bust!"
 He cried in accents wild;
He licked the plates, he sucked the spoons—
 He was a vulgar child.

There came a burst of thunder-sound—
 The boy—oh! where was he?
Ask of the maid who mopped him up,
 The bread crumbs and the tea!

ANONYMOUS

Sir Smashum Uppe

Good afternoon, Sir Smasham Uppe!
We're having tea: do take a cup.
Sugar and milk? Now let me see—
Two lumps, I think? . . . Good gracious me!
The silly thing slipped off your knee!
Pray don't apologize, old chap:
A very trivial mishap!
So clumsy of you? How absurd!
My dear Sir Smasham, not a word!
Now do sit down and have another,
And tell us all about your brother—
You know, the one who broke his head.
Is the poor fellow still in bed?—
A chair—allow me, sir! . . . Great Scott!
That *was* a nasty smash! Eh, what?
Oh, not at all: the chair was old—
Queen Anne, or so we have been told.
We've got at least a dozen more:
Just leave the pieces on the floor.
I want you to admire our view:
Come nearer to the window, do;
And look how beautiful . . . Tut, tut!
You didn't see that it was shut?
I hope you are not badly cut!
Not hurt? A fortunate escape!
Amazing! Not a single scrape!
And now, if you have finished tea,
I fancy you might like to see
A little thing or two I've got.

That china plate? Yes, worth a lot:
A beauty too ... Ah, there it goes!
I trust it didn't hurt your toes?
Your elbow brushed it off the shelf?
Of course: I've done the same myself.
And now, my dear Sir Smasham—Oh,
You surely don't intend to go?
You *must* be off? Well, come again.
So glad you're fond of porcelain!

E. V. RIEU

Doctor Foster

Doctor Foster went to Gloucester
    In a shower of rain;
He stepped in a puddle, up to his middle,
    And never went there again.

NURSERY RHYME

As I Was Going Out One Day

As I was going out one day
My head fell off and rolled away.
But when I saw that it was gone,
I picked it up and put it on.

And when I got into the street
A fellow cried: "Look at your feet!"
I looked at them and sadly said:
"I've left them both asleep in bed!"

ANONYMOUS

Merry Thoughts

Oh, how it makes me giggle
When I think upon the Griggle
And how he used to jiggle
   All up and down the way.
He would always stop and boffle
When he came upon a Squoggle,
I can see him gape and goggle
   As if 'twere yesterday.

But how it makes me chuckle
When I think about the Pruckle,
And how he wore a buckle
   Astride upon his nose;
And how he used to gibber,
To squeak and queak and quibber,
When he felt it sliding downward
   To his webbywistic toes.

But oh! I fairly cackle
When I think about the Knackle,
And how he tried to tackle
   The leaping Limberoo;
It led him such a dance, my dear,
He did not have a chance, my dear,
I hear he fled to France, my dear,
   But that may not be true.

LAURA E. RICHARDS

44

Old Mr. Bows

I'm old Mr. Bows
Whom nobody knows
And my beard is so long that it tickles my toes,
In the front door I shut it.
While I "Tut-tut-tutted"
My wife took a knife and helpfully cut it.
Now I'm old Mr. Bows
With a cold id by dose
And I'll never get warm till my beard again grows
Atishoo!

WILMA HORSBRUGH

Mr. Spats

Mr. Spats
had twenty-six hats
and none of them was the same.
And Mr. Smeds
had twenty-six heads
and only one hat to his name.

Now when Mr. Smeds
met Mr. Spats,
they talked about
buying hats. . . .

And Mr. Spats
bought Mr. Smed's hat!
Did you ever hear
of anything
crazier
than
that?

SHEL SILVERSTEIN

Don't Ever Seize a Weasel by the Tail

You should never squeeze a weasel
for you might displease the weasel,
and don't ever seize a weasel by the tail.

Let his tail blow in the breeze,
if you pull it, he will sneeze
for the weasel's constitution tends to be a little frail.

Yes, the weasel wheezes easily,
the weasel freezes easily,
the weasel's tan complexion rather suddenly turns pale.

So don't displease or tease a weasel,
squeeze or freeze or wheeze a weasel,
and don't ever seize a weasel by the tail, by the tail,
no, don't ever seize a weasel by the tail.

JACK PRELUTSKY

Nursery Nonsense

There lived an old man in a garret,
    So afraid of a little tom-cat,
That he pulled himself up to the ceiling,
    And hung himself up in his hat.

And for fear of the wind and the rain
    He took his umbrella to bed—
I've half an idea that silly old man
    Was a little bit wrong in his head.

D'ARCY WENTWORTH THOMPSON

The Train Pulled in the Station

O, the train pulled in the station,
   The bell was ringing wet;
The track ran by the depot,
   And I think it's running yet.

'Twas midnight on the ocean,
   Not a streetcar was in sight;
The sun and moon were shining,
   And it rained all day that night.

'Twas a summer day in winter,
   And the snow was raining fast;
As a barefoot boy, with shoes on,
   Stood, sitting on the grass.

O, I jumped into the river,
   Just because it had a bed;
I took a sheet of water
   For to cover up my head.

O, the rain makes all things beautiful,
   The flowers and grasses, too;
If the rain makes all things beautiful,
   Why don't it rain on you?

AMERICAN FOLK SONG

Tom Tickleby and His Nose

Little Tom Tickleby,
Answer me quickleby!
   Why is your nose so long?
"I use it," said he,
"For a flute, as you see,
   And it greatly improves my song."

Little Tom Tickleby,
Answer me quickleby!
   Why do you run so fast?
"I am hoping," said he,
"If right swiftly I flee,
   To catch up with my nose at last!"

LAURA E. RICHARDS

Pussy Willow Song

I know a little pussy,
Her coat is silver gray,
She lives out in the meadow,
She'll never run away.
She'll never be a pussy,
She'll never be a cat,
For she's a pussy willow—
Now, what do you think of that?
    Meow, meow, meow, meow,
    Meow, meow, meow, meow. SCAT! !

AMERICAN FOLK SONG

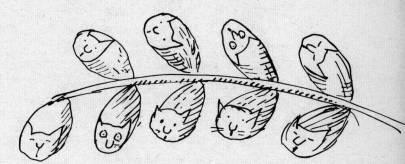

As to the Restless Brook

Do you suppose the babbling brook
    Would stop and rest its head
If someone got a scoop and took
    The pebbles from its bed?

JOHN KENDRICK BANGS

Mr. Kartoffel

Mr. Kartoffel's a whimsical man;
He drinks his beer from a watering can,
And for no good reason that I can see
He fills his pockets with china tea.
He parts his hair with a knife and fork
And takes his ducks for a Sunday walk.
Says he, "If my wife and I should choose
To wear our stockings outside our shoes,
Plant tulip bulbs in the baby's pram
And eat tobacco instead of jam
And fill the bath with cauliflowers,
That's nobody's business at all but ours."
Says Mrs. K.,"I may choose to travel
With a sack of grass or a sack of gravel,
Or paint my toes, one black, one white,
Or sit on a bird's nest half the night—
But whatever I do that is rum or rare,
I rather think that it's my affair.
So fill up your pockets with stamps and string,
And let us be ready for anything!"
Says Mr. K. to his whimsical wife,
"How can we face the storms of life,
Unless we are ready for anything?
So if you've provided the stamps and string,
Let us pump up the saddle and harness the horse
And fill him with carrots and custard and sauce,
Let us leap on him lightly and give him a shove
And it's over the sea and away, my love!"

JAMES REEVE

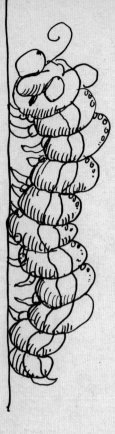

The Tickle Rhyme

"Who's that tickling my back?" said the wall .
"Me," said a small
Caterpillar. "I'm learning
To crawl."

IAN SERRAILLIER

Tragedy

The ship was sailing
   On the sea.
The crew were waiting for their tea.

The ship was tossing
   Up and down.
The toast was getting very brown.

When, suddenly,
   The ship o'erturned,
The toast was *really badly* burned!

W. CHENEY (AGE 10)

Cow

Cows are not supposed to fly,
   And so, if you should see
     A spotted Cow go flying by
      Above a pawpaw tree
In a pork-pie hat with a green umbrella,
   Then run right down the road and tell a
     Lady selling sarsaparilla,
      Lemon soda and vanilla,
So she can come here and tell me!

WILLIAM JAY SMITH

On the Ning Nang Nong

On the Ning Nang Nong
Where the cows go Bong!
And the Monkeys all say Boo!
There's a Nong Nang Ning
Where the trees go Ping!
And the tea pots Jibber Jabber Joo.
On the Nong Ning Nang
All the mice go Clang!
And you just can't catch 'em when they do!
So it's Ning Nang Nong!
Cows go Bong!
Nong Nang Ning!
Trees go Ping!
Nong Ning Nang!
The mice go Clang!
What a noisy place to belong,
Is the Ning Nang Ning Nang Nong!

SPIKE MILLIGAN

alone

A New Song to Sing about Jonathan Bing

O Jonathan Bing, O Bingathon Jon!
Forgets where he's going and thinks he has gone.
He wears his false teeth on the top of his head,
And always stands up when he's sleeping in bed.

O Jonathan Bing has a curious way
Of trying to walk into yesterday,
"If I end with my breakfast and start with my tea,
I *ought* to be able to do it," says he.

O Jonathan Bing is a miser, they say,
For he likes to save trouble and put it away.
"If I never get up in the morning," he said,
"I shall save all the trouble of going to bed!"

"O Jonathan Bing! What a way to behave!
And what do you do with the trouble you save?"
"I wrap it up neatly and send it by post
To my friends and relations who need it the most."

BEATRICE CURTIS BROWN

Tame Animals I Have Known

A thick-fleeced lamb came trotting by:
"Pray whither now, my lamb," quoth I.
"To have," said he with ne'er a stop
"My wool clipped at the baa-baa shop."

I asked the cat: "Pray tell me why
You love to sing?" She blinked her eye.
"My purr-puss, sir, as you can see,
Is to a-mews myself," said she.

NIXON WATERMAN

It Was Shut

"Sam, shut the shutter," Mother Hyde
Called, her cap-strings all a-flutter.
"I've shut the shutter," Sam replied;
"And I can't shut it any shutter."

J. T. GREENLEAF

Jumble Jingle

Pick up a stick up,
    A stick up now pick;
Let me hear you say that
    Nine times, *quick!*

LAURA E. RICHARDS

Order in the Court

Order in the court,
The judge is eating beans.
His wife is in the bathtub
Counting submarines.

JUMP-ROPE RHYME

Fooba Wooba John

Saw a flea kick a tree,
Fooba wooba, fooba wooba,
Saw a flea kick a tree,
Fooba wooba John.
Saw a flea kick a tree
In the middle of the sea,
Fooba wooba, fooba wooba,
Fooba wooba John.

Saw a crow flying low,
Fooba wooba, fooba wooba,
Saw a crow flying low,
Fooba wooba John.
Saw a crow flying low
Several miles beneath the snow,
Fooba wooba, fooba wooba,
Fooba wooba John.

Saw a bug give a shrug . . .
In the middle of the rug . . .

Saw a whale chase a snail . . .
All around a water pail . . .

Saw two geese making cheese . . .
One would hold and the other would squeeze . . .

Saw a mule teaching school . . .
To some bullfrogs in the pool . . .

Saw a bee off to sea . . .
With his fiddle across his knee . . .

Saw a hare chase a deer . . .
Ran it all of seven year . . .

Saw a bear scratch his ear . . .
Wonderin' what we're doing here . . .

'Tis Midnight

'Tis midnight, and the setting sun
    Is slowly rising in the west;
The rapid rivers slowly run,
    The frog is on his downy nest.
The pensive goat and sportive cow
    Hilarious, leap from bough to bough.

ANONYMOUS

Beg Parding

"Beg parding, Mrs. Harding,
Is my kitting in your garding?"
"Is *your* kitting in *my* garding?
Yes she is, and all alone,
Chewing of a mutting bone."

ENGLISH CHILDREN'S RHYME

The Buffalo

The Buffalo, the Buffalo,
He had a horrid snuffle, oh!
And not a single Indian chief
Would lend the beast a handkerchief,
Which shows how very, very far
From courtesy those people are.

LAURA E. RICHARDS

Mister Punchinello

Mother, I want to be married
To Mister Punchinello,
To Mister Punch, to Mister Chin, to Mister
   Nell, to Mister Lo,
Pun—Chin—Nell—Lo—
To Mister Punchinello!

ENGLISH CHILDREN'S RHYME

Good King Wenceslas

Good King Wenceslas looked out
On a cabbage garden:
He bumped into a Brussels sprout
And said "I beg your pardon."

ENGLISH CHILDREN'S STREET RHYME

The Frog

What a wonderful bird the frog are—
When he stand he sit almost;
When he hop, he fly almost.
He ain't got no sense hardly;
He ain't got no tail hardly either.
When he sit, he sit on what he ain't got almost.

ANONYMOUS

Author Index

Title Index